To

....

From

....

Date

....

All things are possible to one who believes,
Yet more to one who hopes,
More still to one who loves,
And most of all to one who practices
And perseveres in all three virtues.

Brother Lawrence

My
Heart-Shaped
Life

Inspirational Journal

My Heart-Shaped Life

Inspirational Journal

KAREN MOORE

SHILOH RUN  PRESS
An Imprint of Barbour Publishing, Inc.

Scripture quotations marked NIV are taken from the HOLY BIBLE, NEW INTERNATIONAL VERSION®. NIV®. Copyright © 1973, 1978, 1984, 2011 by Biblica, Inc.™ Used by permission. All rights reserved.

Scripture quotations marked NCV are taken from the New Century Version of the Bible, copyright © 2005 by Thomas Nelson, Inc. Used by permission. All rights reserved.

Scripture quotations marked NLT are taken from the *Holy Bible*. New Living Translation copyright© 1996, 2004, 2015 by Tyndale House Foundation. Used by permission of Tyndale House Publishers, Inc. Carol Stream, Illinois 60188. All rights reserved.

Scripture quotations marked NKJV are taken from the New King James Version®. Copyright © 1982 by Thomas Nelson, Inc. Used by permission. All rights reserved.

Published by Shiloh Run Press, an imprint of Barbour Publishing, Inc., 1810 Barbour Drive, Uhrichsville, Ohio 44683, www.shilohrunpress.com

Our mission is to inspire the world with the life-changing message of the Bible.

ECPA Member of the Evangelical Christian Publishers Association

Printed in China.

Dear Friends,

This is the day the Lord has made, and God is excited to see what the two of you might do together. He knows your heart. He knows the things that bring you joy and the things that fill you with anxiety.

Use this journal to share your thoughts with God and to remind yourself of all that He has already done in your life. Allow your journaling time to create opportunities to discover more of what God has for you right now. Give yourself permission to dream big dreams as you send steadfast prayers and praise heavenward.

In the days and weeks ahead, you'll be able to look back and see the hand of God at work in your daily life and how He has guided your steps and walked with you each day.

This is the day the Lord has made, and you have every reason to rejoice and be glad in it!

May God bless you and keep you and help you to live a heart-shaped life.

With love and joy,
Karen Moore

If I had the gift of prophecy, and if I understood all of God's secret plans and possessed all knowledge, and if I had such a faith that I could move mountains, but didn't love others, I would be nothing.

1 CORINTHIANS 13:2 NLT

1 Corinthians 13:2 means. . .

My Prayer for a Heart-Shaped Life

Lord, I know my future is in Your hands. . .

....
....
....
....
....
....
....
....
....
....
....
....
....
....
....
....
....
....

A Heart-Shaped View

When my heart is open to God's guidance,
we share beautiful moments together.

Now faith is the substance of things hoped for,
the evidence of things not seen.

HEBREWS 11:1 NKJV

Hebrews 11:1 means. . .

My Prayer for a Heart-Shaped Life

Lord, please help my faith to grow. . .

....

....

....

....

....

....

....

....

....

....

....

....

....

....

....

....

....

....

....

A Heart-Shaped View

There is no love without hope,
No hope without love,
And neither hope nor love without faith.

AUGUSTINE OF HIPPO

Above all else, guard your heart,
for everything you do flows from it.

PROVERBS 4:23 NIV

Proverbs 4:23 means. . .

My Prayer for a Heart-Shaped Life

Lord, keep me always aware of matters of the heart. . .

A Heart-Shaped View

God carries your heart on His sleeve.

Listen to my voice in the morning, Lord. Each morning
I bring my requests to you and wait expectantly.

PSALM 5:3 NLT

Psalm 5:3 means. . .

....

....

....

....

....

....

....

....

....

....

....

....

....

....

....

....

....

....

....

....

My Prayer for a Heart-Shaped Life

Father in heaven, my request to You today is. . .

....

....

....

....

....

....

....

....

....

....

....

....

....

....

....

....

....

A Heart-Shaped View

God loves each one of us as if there were only one of us to love.

AUGUSTINE OF HIPPO

I will give you a new heart and put a new spirit within you;
I will take the heart of stone out of your
flesh and give you a heart of flesh.

EZEKIEL 36:26 NKJV

Ezekiel 36:26 means. . .

My Prayer for a Heart-Shaped Life

Lord, You have blessed my life and made me whole. Help me to. . .

_____

_____

_____

_____

_____

_____

_____

_____

_____

_____

_____

_____

_____

_____

_____

_____

_____

_____

_____

A Heart-Shaped View

For the love of God is broader
Than the measures of man's mind;
And the heart of the Eternal
Is most wonderfully kind.

F. W. FABER

Plans fail for lack of counsel,
but with many advisers they succeed.

PROVERBS 15:22 NIV

Proverbs 15:22 means. . .

My Prayer for a Heart-Shaped Life

Lord, I need Your guidance about. . .

A Heart-Shaped View

Do not open your heart to everyone, but discuss
your affairs with one who is wise and who fears God.

THOMAS À KEMPIS

And He said to me, "My grace is sufficient for you,
for My strength is made perfect in weakness."
2 CORINTHIANS 12:9 NKJV

2 Corinthians 12:9 means. . .

My Prayer for a Heart-Shaped Life

*Lord, I turn everything I am—and all that I have—
over to You. Give me strength to. . .*

A Heart-Shaped View

God loves us not because of who we are,
But because of who *He* is.
UNKNOWN

....
....
....
....
....
....
....
....
....
....
....
....
....
....
....
....

Wait on the LORD;
Be of good courage,
And He shall strengthen your heart;
Wait, I say, on the LORD!

PSALM 27:14 NKJV

Psalm 27:14 means. . .

_____

_____

_____

_____

_____

_____

_____

_____

_____

_____

_____

_____

_____

_____

_____

_____

_____

_____

_____

My Prayer for a Heart-Shaped Life

Lord, please help me to wait on You for. . .

....

....

....

....

....

....

....

....

....

....

....

....

....

....

....

....

....

....

A Heart-Shaped View

It is the heart which perceives
God and not the reason.

BLAISE PASCAL

And do not be conformed to this world, but be transformed by the renewing of your mind, that you may prove what is that good and acceptable and perfect will of God.

ROMANS 12:2 NKJV

Romans 12:2 means. . .

....
....
....
....
....
....
....
....
....
....
....
....
....
....
....
....
....
....
....
....
....
....
....

My Prayer for a Heart-Shaped Life

Dear God, renew my mind and my heart and help me to. . .

_____

_____

_____

_____

_____

_____

_____

_____

_____

_____

_____

_____

_____

_____

_____

_____

_____

_____

_____

A Heart-Shaped View

Neither prayer nor praise,
nor the hearing of the Word
will be profitable to those
who have left their hearts behind them.

C. H. SPURGEON

"I say this because I know what I am planning for you," says the LORD. *"I have good plans for you, not plans to hurt you. I will give you hope and a good future."*

JEREMIAH 29:11 NCV

Jeremiah 29:11 means. . .

My Prayer for a Heart-Shaped Life

Lord, help me to draw near to You and to know Your plans so I can. . .

....

....

....

....

....

....

....

....

....

....

....

....

....

....

....

....

....

....

....

....

A Heart-Shaped View

To hold to God is to rely on the fact that God
is there for me, and to live in this certainty.

KARL BARTH

*"Lord, remind me how brief my time on earth will be.
Remind me that my days are numbered—how fleeting my life is."*

PSALM 39:4 NLT

Psalm 39:4 means. . .

My Prayer for a Heart-Shaped Life

Father, let me remember today to. . .

A Heart-Shaped View

Look to this day. . .yesterday is but a dream, and tomorrow is only
a vision. But today, well-lived, makes every yesterday a dream
of happiness and every tomorrow a vision of hope.

UNKNOWN

Rejoice always, pray continually, give thanks in all circumstances; for this is God's will for you in Christ Jesus.

1 THESSALONIANS 5:16–18 NIV

1 Thessalonians 5:16–18 means. . .

My Prayer for a Heart-Shaped Life

Lord, I thank You for...

....

....

....

....

....

....

....

....

....

....

....

....

....

....

....

....

....

....

A Heart-Shaped View

A thankful heart is not only the greatest virtue,
but the parent of all other virtues.

CICERO

My flesh and my heart may fail, but God is
the strength of my heart and my portion forever.

PSALM 73:26 NIV

Psalm 73:26 means. . .

My Prayer for a Heart-Shaped Life

Lord, thank You for giving me strength to. . .

A Heart-Shaped View

The way to grow strong in Christ is to grow weak in yourself.
C. H. Spurgeon

"May the LORD bless you and keep you. May the LORD show you his kindness and have mercy on you. May the LORD watch over you and give you peace."

NUMBERS 6:24–26 NCV

....

....

....

....

....

....

....

....

....

....

....

....

....

....

....

....

....

....

....

....

....

Numbers 6:24–26 means. . .

My Prayer for a Heart-Shaped Life

Lord, please watch over me as I...

A Heart-Shaped View

God is more anxious to bestow His blessings
on us than we are to receive them.

AUGUSTINE OF HIPPO

Bear with each other and forgive one another if any of you has a grievance against someone. Forgive as the Lord forgave you.

COLOSSIANS 3:13 NIV

Colossians 3:13 means. . .

My Prayer for a Heart-Shaped Life

Lord, I ask You to help me be forgiving toward. . .

....

....

....

....

....

....

....

....

....

....

....

....

....

....

....

....

A Heart-Shaped View

When you forgive, you do not change the past,
but you most surely change the future.

BERNARD MELTZER

The LORD looks down from heaven and sees the whole human race.
From his throne he observes all who live on the earth. He made
their hearts, so he understands everything they do.

PSALM 33:13–15 NLT

Psalm 33:13–15 means. . .

My Prayer for a Heart-Shaped Life

Lord, thank You for understanding me so well. Help me to. . .

_____

_____

_____

_____

_____

_____

_____

_____

_____

_____

_____

_____

_____

_____

_____

_____

_____

_____

A Heart-Shaped View

There are two kinds of people:
Those who say to God, "Thy will be done!"
And those to whom God says,
"All right then, have it your way."

C. S. Lewis

....

....

....

....

....

....

....

....

....

....

....

....

....

....

....

Acknowledge the God of your Father and serve him with wholehearted devotion and with a willing mind, for the LORD searches every heart and understands every desire and every thought. If you seek him, he will be found by you.

1 CHRONICLES 28:9 NIV

1 Chronicles 28:9 means. . .

My Prayer for a Heart-Shaped Life

Lord, I seek You today as I. . .

A Heart-Shaped View

A loving heart is the truest wisdom.

CHARLES DICKENS

"I give you a new command: Love each other. You must love each other as I have loved you. All people will know that you are my followers if you love each other."

JOHN 13:34–35 NCV

John 13:34–35 means. . .

_____

_____

_____

_____

_____

_____

_____

_____

_____

_____

_____

_____

_____

_____

_____

_____

_____

_____

My Prayer for a Heart-Shaped Life

Lord, help me to be more loving toward. . .

....

....

....

....

....

....

....

....

....

....

....

....

....

....

....

....

....

....

A Heart-Shaped View

Love is the sum of all virtue, and love disposes us to do good.
JONATHAN EDWARDS

"Do to others as you would have them do to you."

LUKE 6:31 NIV

Luke 6:31 means. . .

My Prayer for a Heart-Shaped Life

Lord, let me always be an example of Your love and. . .

....

....

....

....

....

....

....

....

....

....

....

....

....

....

....

....

....

....

....

....

A Heart-Shaped View

Love is all we have, the only way that we each can help the other.

EURIPIDES

This is the day the LORD has made;
We will rejoice and be glad in it.

PSALM 118:24 NKJV

Psalm 118:24 means. . .

My Prayer for a Heart-Shaped Life

Lord, today I thank You for the blessing of. . .

....

....

....

....

....

....

....

....

....

....

....

....

....

....

....

....

....

....

A Heart-Shaped View

He who gives you the day will also
give you the things necessary for the day.

GREGORY OF NYSSA

I will praise you, LORD, with all my heart;
I will tell of all the marvelous things you have done.
I will be filled with joy because of you.
I will sing praises to your name, O Most High.

PSALM 9:1–2 NLT

Psalm 9:1–2 means. . .

My Prayer for a Heart-Shaped Life

Lord, I give You thanks and praise for. . .

A Heart-Shaped View

Praising God is one of the highest and purest acts of religion.
In prayer, we act like human beings; in praise, we act like angels.

THOMAS WATSON

But the plans of the LORD stand firm forever,
the purposes of his heart through all generations.
PSALM 33:11 NIV

Psalm 33:11 means. . .

My Prayer for a Heart-Shaped Life

Lord, I pray to fulfill Your purpose for me through. . .

A Heart-Shaped View

The only possible answer to the destiny of human beings
is to seek continually to fulfill God's purpose.

P. TOURNIER

"You must not hate your fellow citizen in your heart. If your neighbor does something wrong, tell him about it, or you will be partly to blame. Forget about the wrong things people do to you, and do not try to get even. Love your neighbor as you love yourself."

LEVITICUS 19:17–18 NCV

Leviticus 19:17–18 means. . .

My Prayer for a Heart-Shaped Life

*Heavenly Father, teach me the ways I can be
better at loving those around me, particularly. . .*

....

....

....

....

....

....

....

....

....

....

....

....

....

....

....

....

....

....

A Heart-Shaped View

The love of God is the first and great commandment.
But love of our neighbor is how we obey it.

AUGUSTINE OF HIPPO

> *"I leave you peace; my peace I give you. I do not give it to you as the world does. So don't let your hearts be troubled or afraid."*
>
> JOHN 14:27 NCV

John 14:27 means. . .

_____
_____
_____
_____
_____
_____
_____
_____
_____
_____
_____
_____
_____
_____
_____
_____
_____
_____
_____
_____

My Prayer for a Heart-Shaped Life

Lord, help me to trust You in every area of my life, especially...

....

....

....

....

....

....

....

....

....

....

....

....

....

....

....

....

....

....

....

A Heart-Shaped View

What peace and inward quiet should we have if we would cut
away all busyness of mind and think only on heavenly things.

THOMAS À KEMPIS

And now abide faith, hope, love, these three;
but the greatest of these is love.

1 CORINTHIANS 13:13 NKJV

1 Corinthians 13:13 means. . .

My Prayer for a Heart-Shaped Life

Lord, I thank You for all the ways You show me Your love, especially. . .

....

....

....

....

....

....

....

....

....

....

....

....

....

....

....

....

....

....

A Heart-Shaped View

You learn to love by loving.

FRANCIS DE SALES

Know in your heart that the LORD *your*
God corrects you as a parent corrects a child.
DEUTERONOMY 8:5 NCV

Deuteronomy 8:5 means. . .

My Prayer for a Heart-Shaped Life

Lord, thank You for guiding me to change. . .

A Heart-Shaped View

Courage is the strength or choice to begin a change.
Determination is the persistence to continue in that change.

UNKNOWN

The group of believers were united in their hearts and spirit.
All those in the group acted as though their private property
belonged to everyone in the group. In fact, they shared everything.

ACTS 4:32 NCV

Acts 4:32 means. . .

....

....

....

....

....

....

....

....

....

....

....

....

....

....

....

....

....

....

....

....

....

....

My Prayer for a Heart-Shaped Life

*Lord, help me to be more open to sharing my story with others,
especially when it comes to. . .*

A Heart-Shaped View

Give strength, give thought, give deeds, give wealth;
Give love, give tears, and give yourself.
Give, give, be always giving,
Who gives not, is not living,
The more you give, the more you live.

UNKNOWN

"[God,] forgive and treat each person as he should be treated because you know what is in a person's heart. Only you know what is in everyone's heart."

1 KINGS 8:39 NCV

1 Kings 8:39 means. . .

My Prayer for a Heart-Shaped Life

Lord, thank You for knowing my heart and helping me to. . .

....

....

....

....

....

....

....

....

....

....

....

....

....

....

....

....

....

....

....

A Heart-Shaped View

Humanity is never so beautiful as when praying
for forgiveness or else forgiving one another.

JEAN PAUL RICHTER

*In the past, people did not understand God,
and he ignored this. But now, God tells all people
in the world to change their hearts and lives.*

ACTS 17:30 NCV

Acts 17:30 means. . .

_____
_____
_____
_____
_____
_____
_____
_____
_____
_____
_____
_____
_____
_____
_____
_____
_____
_____
_____

My Prayer for a Heart-Shaped Life

Lord, please help me change my heart in the way I...

....
....
....
....
....
....
....
....
....
....
....
....
....
....
....
....
....
....
....

A Heart-Shaped View

Live in the world as if God and your soul were the only things that existed; so that your heart cannot be made captive to any earthly thing.

JOHN OF THE CROSS

"I ask that you give me a heart that understands, so I can rule the people in the right way and will know the difference between right and wrong. Otherwise, it is impossible to rule this great people of yours."

1 Kings 3:9 NCV

1 Kings 3:9 means. . .

My Prayer for a Heart-Shaped Life

Father, I ask that wisdom would rule over my life today as I. . .

A Heart-Shaped View

You can have knowledge without having wisdom,
but you cannot have wisdom without having knowledge.

R. C. SPROUL

"God does not see the same way people see. People look at the outside of a person, but the LORD looks at the heart."

1 SAMUEL 16:7 NCV

1 Samuel 16:7 means. . .

My Prayer for a Heart-Shaped Life

Lord, thank You for seeing me "heart first" today. . .

....

....

....

....

....

....

....

....

....

....

....

....

....

....

....

....

....

....

....

....

A Heart-Shaped View

See that your chief study be about your heart:
That there God's image may be planted,
That there His interests be advanced,
That there the world and flesh are subdued,
That there the love of every sin is cast out;
That there the love of holiness grows.

JONATHAN EDWARDS

God protects me like a shield;
he saves those whose hearts are right.
PSALM 7:10 NCV

Psalm 7:10 means. . .

....

....

....

....

....

....

....

....

....

....

....

....

....

....

....

....

....

....

....

....

....

....

....

My Prayer for a Heart-Shaped Life

Lord, help me to live a more heart-shaped life as I. . .

....

....

....

....

....

....

....

....

....

....

....

....

....

....

....

....

....

....

....

A Heart-Shaped View

To my God a heart of flame;
To humanity a heart of love;
To myself, a heart of steel.

AUGUSTINE OF HIPPO

Don't ever forget kindness and truth. Wear them like a necklace. Write them on your heart as if on a tablet.

PROVERBS 3:3 NCV

Proverbs 3:3 means. . .

My Prayer for a Heart-Shaped Life

Lord, let me always take note of being kind, especially when. . .

A Heart-Shaped View

Spread love everywhere you go: first of all in your own house.
Let no one ever come to you without leaving better and
happier. Be the living expression of God's kindness.

MOTHER TERESA

The purpose of my instruction is that all believers would be filled with love that comes from a pure heart, a clear conscience, and genuine faith.

1 TIMOTHY 1:5 NLT

1 Timothy 1:5 means. . .

My Prayer for a Heart-Shaped Life

Father, I pray that I would love others with a pure heart. Help me to. . .

A Heart-Shaped View

Far away there in the sunshine are my highest aspirations.
I may not reach them, but I can look up and see their beauty,
believe in them, and try to follow where they lead.

LOUISA MAY ALCOTT

*"You must give your whole heart to him
and hold out your hands to him for help."*

JOB 11:13 NCV

Job 11:13 means. . .

....
....
....
....
....
....
....
....
....
....
....
....
....
....
....
....
....
....
....
....
....
....
....

My Prayer for a Heart-Shaped Life

Lord, today I raise my hands to You and pray for. . .

....

....

....

....

....

....

....

....

....

....

....

....

....

....

....

....

....

....

....

....

....

A Heart-Shaped View

The reason why we obtain no more in prayer is because we expect
no more. God usually answers us according to our own hearts.

RICHARD ALLEINE

He answered, "'Love the Lord your God with all your heart and with all your soul and with all your strength and with all your mind'; and, 'Love your neighbor as yourself.'"

LUKE 10:27 NIV

Luke 10:27 means. . .

My Prayer for a Heart-Shaped Life

Lord, open my heart to love You more, especially when. . .

_____

_____

_____

_____

_____

_____

_____

_____

_____

_____

_____

_____

_____

_____

_____

_____

_____

_____

A Heart-Shaped View

Love is the fulfillment of all our works.
There is the goal: that is why we run:
We run toward it, and once we reach it,
in it, we shall find rest.

AUGUSTINE OF HIPPO

"That person's heart blessed me, because I warmed him with the wool of my sheep."

JOB 31:20 NCV

Job 31:20 means. . .

....
....
....
....
....
....
....
....
....
....
....
....
....
....
....
....
....
....
....
....
....
....

My Prayer for a Heart-Shaped Life

Lord, grant that I might cause just one person to smile today because. . .

A Heart-Shaped View

If I can stop one heart from breaking,
I shall not live in vain;
If I can ease one life the aching,
Or cool one pain,
Or help one fainting robin,
Unto his nest again,
I shall not live in vain.

EMILY DICKINSON

Trust the LORD with all your heart,
and don't depend on your own understanding.
PROVERBS 3:5 NCV

Proverbs 3:5 means. . .

My Prayer for a Heart-Shaped Life

Lord, help me to trust You more in the matter of. . .

....

....

....

....

....

....

....

....

....

....

....

....

....

....

....

....

....

....

....

....

....

....

....

....

A Heart-Shaped View

Trust the past to God's mercy,
The present to God's love,
And the future to God's providence.

AUGUSTINE OF HIPPO

So continuing daily with one accord in the temple, and breaking bread from house to house, they ate their food with gladness and simplicity of heart, praising God and having favor with all the people.

ACTS 2:46–47 NKJV

Acts 2:46–47 means. . .

_____

_____

_____

_____

_____

_____

_____

_____

_____

_____

_____

_____

_____

_____

_____

_____

_____

_____

_____

_____

_____

My Prayer for a Heart-Shaped Life

*Lord, thank You for all the people You have brought
together to serve You, especially. . .*

A Heart-Shaped View

You will find, as you look back upon your life, that the moments that stand out are the moments when you have done things for others.

HENRY DRUMMOND

The teachings of their God are in their heart,
so they do not fail to keep them.
PSALM 37:31 NCV

Psalm 37:31 means. . .

My Prayer for a Heart-Shaped Life

*Lord, thank You for allowing my heart to know
You and for giving me enough love to. . .*

....

....

....

....

....

....

....

....

....

....

....

....

....

....

....

....

....

....

A Heart-Shaped View

God doesn't call the equipped. He equips the called.
UNKNOWN

Now hope does not disappoint, because the love of God has been poured out in our hearts by the Holy Spirit who was given to us.

ROMANS 5:5 NKJV

Romans 5:5 means. . .

My Prayer for a Heart-Shaped Life

Dear Lord, You have filled my heart with hope today for. . .

....
....
....
....
....
....
....
....
....
....
....
....
....
....
....
....
....
....
....
....

A Heart-Shaped View

If it were not for hopes, the heart would break.

THOMAS FULLER

Every day is hard for those who suffer,
but a happy heart is like a continual feast.

PROVERBS 15:15 NCV

Proverbs 15:15 means. . .

My Prayer for a Heart-Shaped Life

Oh God, help me to celebrate all the good in my life, especially. . .

....

....

....

....

....

....

....

....

....

....

....

....

....

....

....

....

A Heart-Shaped View

The happiness for which our souls ache is one undisturbed
by success or failure, one which will root deeply inside us
and give inward relaxation, peace and contentment,
no matter what the surface problems may be.

BILLY GRAHAM

The sacrifice God wants is a broken spirit. God,
you will not reject a heart that is broken and sorry for sin.

PSALM 51:17 NCV

Psalm 51:17 means. . .

My Prayer for a Heart-Shaped Life

God, my heart is broken today for. . .

....

....

....

....

....

....

....

....

....

....

....

....

....

....

....

....

....

....

A Heart-Shaped View

To handle yourself, use your head.
To handle others, use your heart.

UNKNOWN

....

....

....

....

....

....

....

....

....

....

....

....

....

....

....

....

I do not hide your goodness in my heart;
I speak about your loyalty and salvation.
I do not hide your love and truth from the people. . .

PSALM 40:10 NCV

Psalm 40:10 means. . .

My Prayer for a Heart-Shaped Life

Lord, I am grateful to share stories of my faith.
Help me to share my faith with. . .

A Heart-Shaped View

A little faith will bring your soul to heaven,
but a lot of faith will bring heaven to your soul.

DWIGHT L. MOODY

....

....

....

....

....

....

....

....

....

....

....

....

....

....

....

....

Put me like a seal on your heart,
like a seal on your arm.
SONG OF SOLOMON 8:6 NCV

Song of Solomon 8:6 means. . .

My Prayer for a Heart-Shaped Life

Lord, thank You for drawing me close to You.
I seek Your faithfulness as I. . .

....

....

....

....

....

....

....

....

....

....

....

....

....

....

....

....

....

A Heart-Shaped View

God shows Himself not to reason, but to faith and love.
A. W. Tozer

Your lives are a letter written in our hearts; everyone can read it and recognize our good work among you. Clearly, you are a letter from Christ showing the result of our ministry among you.

2 CORINTHIANS 3:2–3 NLT

2 Corinthians 3:2-3 means. . .

My Prayer for a Heart-Shaped Life

Dear God, help me write Your story on my heart and share it with. . .

....

....

....

....

....

....

....

....

....

....

....

....

....

....

....

....

....

....

....

....

....

....

A Heart-Shaped View

Be careful how you live. You may be the
only Bible some people ever read.

BILLY GRAHAM

Create in me a pure heart, God,
and make my spirit right again.
PSALM 51:10 NCV

Psalm 51:10 means. . .

_____

_____

_____

_____

_____

_____

_____

_____

_____

_____

_____

_____

_____

_____

_____

_____

_____

_____

_____

_____

_____

My Prayer for a Heart-Shaped Life

Lord, please heal me with Your love, especially when it comes to. . .

....

....

....

....

....

....

....

....

....

....

....

....

....

....

....

....

....

....

....

....

....

A Heart-Shaped View

Spirit-filled souls are ablaze for God.
They love with a love that glows.

SAMUEL CHADWICK

*"I give new life to those who are humble
and to those whose hearts are broken."*

ISAIAH 57:15 NCV

Isaiah 57:15 means. . .

My Prayer for a Heart-Shaped Life

Father, please rescue me. My heart breaks for...

....

....

....

....

....

....

....

....

....

....

....

....

....

....

....

....

....

....

A Heart-Shaped View

God can do wonders with a broken
heart if we give Him all the pieces.

UNKNOWN

Be filled with the Holy Spirit, singing psalms and hymns and spiritual songs among yourselves, and making music to the Lord in your hearts.

EPHESIANS 5:18–19 NLT

Ephesians 5:18–19 means. . .

_____
_____
_____
_____
_____
_____
_____
_____
_____
_____
_____
_____
_____
_____
_____
_____
_____
_____
_____
_____
_____

My Prayer for a Heart-Shaped Life

Lord, I sing to You today with joy because...

....

....

....

....

....

....

....

....

....

....

....

....

....

....

....

....

....

....

....

....

....

....

A Heart-Shaped View

God respects me when I work, but He loves me when I sing!

Rabindranath Tagore

You will search for me. And when you search for me with all your heart, you will find me!

JEREMIAH 29:13 NCV

Jeremiah 29:13 means. . .

My Prayer for a Heart-Shaped Life

Father, I am seeking You with all my heart today because. . .

A Heart-Shaped View

We pursue God because, and only because, He has
put an urge within us that spurs us to that pursuit.

A. W. Tozer

*Do the things that show you really
have changed your hearts and lives.*
MATTHEW 3:8 NCV

Matthew 3:8 means. . .

My Prayer for a Heart-Shaped Life

Lord, help me to show that my heart belongs to You in the ways I. . .

_____

_____

_____

_____

_____

_____

_____

_____

_____

_____

_____

_____

_____

_____

_____

_____

_____

A Heart-Shaped View

Our Lord does not care so much for the importance of
our works as for the love with which they are done.

TERESA OF AVILA

It is good for you to follow closely what they said as you would follow a light shining in a dark place, until the day begins and the morning star rises in your hearts.

2 PETER 1:19 NCV

2 Peter 1:19 means. . .

My Prayer for a Heart-Shaped Life

Lord, help me to follow You in word and deed by. . .

A Heart-Shaped View

It is only with the heart that one can see rightly;
what is essential is invisible to the eye.

ANTOINE DE SAINT-EXUPÉRY

So this is what the LORD says: "If you change your heart and return to me, I will take you back. Then you may serve me."

JEREMIAH 15:19 NCV

Jeremiah 15:19 means. . .

My Prayer for a Heart-Shaped Life

Father in heaven, help me to return to You with my whole heart as I...

A Heart-Shaped View

God will put up with a great many things in the human heart,
but there is one thing He will not put up with. . .a second place.

JOHN RUSKIN

"Good people have good things in their hearts, and so they say good things."

MATTHEW 12:35 NCV

Matthew 12:35 means. . .

....

....

....

....

....

....

....

....

....

....

....

....

....

....

....

....

....

....

....

....

My Prayer for a Heart-Shaped Life

Lord, help me to share kind words with those around me, especially. . .

A Heart-Shaped View

Words which do not give the light of Christ increase the darkness.

MOTHER TERESA

Living a Heart-Shaped Life

Joy is love exalted;
Peace is love in repose;
Long-suffering is love enduring;
Gentleness is love in society;
Goodness is love in action;
Faith is love on the battlefield;
Meekness is love in school;
And temperance is love in training.

D. L. MOODY